Developing Social Intelligence

90 Minute Guides

Michelle N. Halsey

Silver City Publications & Training, L.L.C.
P.O. Box 1914
Nampa, ID 83653
https://www.silvercitypublications.com/shop/

ISBN-10: 1-64004-019-6
ISBN-13: 978-1-64004-019-9

Contents

Chapter 1 – Increase Your Self Awareness

Social intelligence can seem like a complicated term and can make many of us feel nervous. But social intelligence is something we deal with every day and it can help us navigate better experiences from our social environment. Whether we're at home or at work, knowing how to be more aware of ourselves and our surroundings can help us make the best out of any social situation!

At the end of this guide, you should be able to:

- Be aware of our own behaviors

- Learn to be empathetic with others

- Know tools for active listening

- Effectively communicate interpersonally

- Recognize various social cues

- Determine appropriate conversation topics

- Know various forms of body language

Before reading this chapter, answer the following questions.

1. In your own words, what is social intelligence? Have you ever heard this term before?

2. Why is social intelligence important at home and work?

3. What areas of social intelligence would you be more interested in learning about?

4. What do you hope to learn or take away from this class?

Many times we wonder why the situations around us change simply because we are relying on the people around us to change. But being aware of our own actions and behaviors is one of the key tools to change not only ourselves, but our surroundings. We must be aware of what communication we are putting out there and how our behaviors can affect others.

Remove or Limit Self-Deception

Self-deception is a tool we commonly use to try and hide something from ourselves or prevent ourselves from accepting something. We can often try to make ourselves believe whatever we want and alter facts in our mind by self-deceiving ourselves. No one is exempt from this habit and we can find ourselves practicing it more often than we think. For instance, we can self-deceive ourselves that our presentation was the best in the group or self-deceive ourselves to believe that people are talking about us when we walk away. It can affect our relationships with others and give people the wrong impression of ourselves. One of the simplest ways we can help prevent this type of deception is to simply be direct with ourselves and others.

Always say what you mean and mean what you say – don't try to deceive with alternative phrases or meanings. When taking in information, review it over before making conclusions. Recognize facts and happenings that could form a final thought. For instance, your presentation may have been very good, but do not assume it was the best out of the group. While it is alright to build confidence and esteem by believing in yourself or believing you know what is best, it is not beneficial to deceive ourselves into thinking over the line since it can cause us to damage our future relationships with others.

Ask For Feedback

We often forget one of the easiest tools to increase our own self-awareness is to simply ask for feedback from those around us. It doesn't have to be a lengthy or complicated process and can be done very professionally or casually. The people around us can see our usual actions and behaviors and can give an honest opinion about them. The thought of asking someone to share their opinions and thoughts about us can seem unnerving and even downright scary, but the advice and thoughts can prove invaluable. If possible, let the person know in advance you will want feedback later so they have time to form an impression and gather any tips or hints. A random request for feedback (such as right after a meeting) can be acceptable too, but keep in mind the person may be caught off guard and will not be able to give a good answer right away.

The most important part about asking for feedback it to prepare yourself for what you may hear. Not all feedback is positive. Take the advice and tips that the person offers as tools to help you improve yourself and style. Don't turn defensive or angry just because the person delivering the feedback may have said something you don't particularly want to hear.

Be Open to Change

Humans are designed to be creatures of habit. We often have the mindset of "we want what we want when we want it", and if something throws a kink in our routine, we can go a little crazy sometimes. But being open to change allows us to adapt to new surroundings and situations and helps us grow as a person. Changing our attitude about ourselves and others can help determine how we build our connections. Sometimes after we receive feedback from our peers, we may need to change how we do things or behave in a group. Perhaps after a meeting we decide we need to change how we plan our presentations. Whatever the reason, it is important to not disregard the importance of your willingness to change and not turn a blind eye to its prospects. Changing how we see ourselves and the people that surround us can have a positive impact on our attitudes and can help build better relationships with our peers.

Tips for accepting change:

- Determine how the change can benefit you

- Don't assume a need for change is negative

- Recognize that change is a chance for improvement

Reflect On Your Actions

While feedback from other people can be a great tool to use, feedback from ourselves can be just as valuable (without being self-deceptive). Being reflective gives us a chance to learn from our past experiences (even our mistakes) and recognize the chance for learning opportunities. By reflecting on our actions, we can see firsthand what actions we took, how they played out, and what kind of effect they had on people. Use all of your senses to recreate an experience in your mind and the actions that you took. What behaviors did you show? What did you feel at the time? What type of reactions did you receive from other people?

Reflect back on any body language cues you may have used and make note of any cues you may have seen in others. What intuitions or gut feelings do you feel from the experience? Do you feel as though you have learned anything new from the experience? These steps and process can help you reflect back on your actions and increase not only your self-awareness, but your awareness of others.

Chapter 2 – The Keys to Empathy

Empathy is one of our greatest interpersonal skills because it allows us to have better communication with people around us and increases our understanding of others. We know empathy can simply mean to 'put ourselves in the other person's shoes', but it can also mean to take an active role in getting to know the people around you and treating them with the respect they deserve.

Listening and Paying Attention

We all know that there is a difference between hearing and listening, but yet we still seem to confuse the two when we communicate with other people. Listening is considered a skill, so like any other skill it must be implemented and strengthened. Listening allows for you to understand what the person is talking about and register what they are trying to communicate. Building better listening skills starts with learning to pay attention when someone speaks and actively listening to what they are saying. Key tips to help accomplish this are to give your attention to the person by facing them and making eye contact. Turn off any cell phones or pagers or remove any item from the area that can distract you and make you lose focus. You'll find that you will catch more of what the person is saying and be able to retain more. Paying attention and building better listening skills can show support for the other person and build rapport with them.

Tips for better listening skills:

- Remove any distractions

- Make eye contact with the person speaking

- Nod your head periodically

- Ask for follow up details or information

- Ask the person to repeat anything you may have missed

Don't Judge

No matter how many times we hear the old phrase "Don't judge people" or "It's not our place to judge", we more than likely find ourselves doing it anyway – we just don't want to admit it. Whether subconsciously or not, we still find ourselves judging those around us, whether it is based on their clothes, job title, the way the talk or walk, gender, hair color, skin color, and etc. When someone is speaking or completes a task, what do you think in your head? Do you automatically make comments on how their assignment was too easy or that the way they speak is subpar to the group. Of course you would never say this out loud or tell them directly, but in your mind you have already made up your mind about them.

Thoughts like this cause us to judge people more and more, which can create barriers between people and lose connections and chances to network over time. Every person has an "inside person" and an "outside person" – we see the outside person every day and try to form our own opinions without seeing everything first. Don't forget that there is an "inside person" as well that has an entirely different side.

Shift Your View

Empathy is simply defined as putting yourself in another person's shoes and seeing things from their point of view. When communicating with another person, think about how it would feel to be in their shoes and do the things they have to do. How would you feel if you have to complete their assignment in the weekly meeting or if you have to conduct a speech in front of hundreds of people?

Shifting your view does not mean that you have to entirely give up your opinions and what you think. It involves taking a few minutes to stop and reflect on the actions and words of the other person and picturing yourself in their situation. Think about what it would be like to stand in their shoes in the conference room or in front of the new manager. By doing this, we can better understand why they may act or speak a certain way and what can drive them to do what they do. By showing empathy, you are able to connect with this person and create an important relationship to have in the workplace.

Don't Show Fake Emotions

In social situations it is never a good idea to fake our emotions or how we feel toward others. Of course, this does not mean we have full permission to start tearing into people and ripping them to shreds if we didn't like their recent speech. But if you are not entirely happy about something in the group or feel anxious about something else, it is not a good idea to fake a smile or laugh just to appear happy.

This 'fakeness' will more than likely be detected, which can offend others around you or even make them feel insecure. Instead, be honest about how you feel and show honest concern for your peers. Be tactful if delivering negative feedback and offers helpful tips for improvement or changes. Although they may not accept your true feelings at first, and may even seem angry about it, in the end they will appreciate the fact that you were honest with them and didn't show a mask of fake emotions with them.

Chapter 3 – Active Listening

It is not always enough to simply listen to a person and have the sense of 'waiting to speak'. This type of listening will cause us to lose out on important information and deny us the chance to make any real connection. By using active listening, we are more inept to learn about other people and take an active interest in what they have to say and offer. This concept can not only improve your overall listening skills, but your overall connections with other people as well.

Attunement

Attunement is defined as being aware and responsive to another person. When developing active listening skills, this tool is used to better connect with the person and become more 'in tune' with what they are saying. Since attunement relies heavily on nonverbal communication (such as body language), it is important to pay attention to the signals that the other person gives off, as well as the ones we use. Key gestures such as smiling, hand gesturing, eye contact and body movement can signal a connection or a break in communication. When we use these gestures toward other people, it can make them feel more connected with us and continue to open up with us. These connections can form bonds that can benefit the both of you and build networks for the future.

Don't Jump to Conclusions

It's a common gesture to hear something or witness someone do something and try to jump to a conclusion about it right away. Maybe you didn't like what they said or heard something you didn't think was appropriate, so you reach conclusions that the person has poor speaking skills or doesn't know how to communicate with others. But this quick acting judgment can only harm your business relationships and misses the chance to really listen to someone and make a connection. While you may believe you have all the facts and have reached a final decision, always remember there is another side of the coin and most likely more information to know.

Even if you in fact do have everything you need, you may still not be able to process his thought in way that can be productive or even helpful to anyone since it is based on negativity. If someone says something that makes you jump to a conclusion, ask them to repeat it or clarify what they said. Then take a few minutes to reflect on what was said or done and take enough time to form a logical conclusion about it. Taking a little extra time may seem like a chore at times, but it can save you from jumping to unnecessary conclusions and ruining the chance to build a relationship with another coworker.

Shift Your Focus

Naturally, we often think of ourselves as Number One. We're the first person we try to take care of and try to guard ourselves when necessary. But when it comes to active listening, the role is often reversed in order to focus on the other person. In order to actively listen, we must shift the focus from ourselves to the person speaking at the time and become attune to what they are saying. Steps should include turning to face the person and making eye contact with them. During the conversation, nod your head periodically and give them time to pause or rest before talking yourself.

When they have finished, stay focused on them by asking questions about what they have said. Don't be afraid to ask them to clarify something you didn't catch or something you may have missed. By shifting your focus to them instead of on your thoughts, you should be able to remember and comprehend most of what was said. From here you can be able to offer suggestions or opinions and engage in open conversation with the person. They'll be more likely to openly share with you if they feel as though you can focus on them as well as yourself.

Don't Discount Feelings

One of the biggest faults many of us have is the need to 'fix' things when we something that has gone wrong. When we get some bad news or information about a bad situation, we often try to follow it up with "It's not so bad" or "It could be worse". While this may seem like a helpful gesture, it can actually cause more damage than good because it makes the other person feel as though their feelings about the situation are invalid or void.

It gives the impression that you are not necessarily listening to the problem, but imply trying to brush it over and discount their feelings altogether. When a person is speaking about something they feel strongly about, whether it is about work or personal situations, it is important to recognize that it is the way they feel and that they are entitled to feel that way. Instead of trying to smooth the problem over, listen to what the person is saying and how they are feeling and offer support. Let them know you are there to help and can always lend an ear. They will appreciate the gesture much more than any half-hearted solution or smooth-over phrase.

Chapter 4 – Insight on Behavior

Behavior can be a complicated concept to try and master, much less understand. Every person is different and can interpret behaviors differently. In social groups, there is a wide range of behaviors occurring, which can seem overwhelming at times. But by having a little insight on not only the behavior others, but our own, we are able to better understand what is going on around us and how to navigate through the situation.

Perception

Perception can be a hard aspect to learn from since most of the time our perception can only be drawn from our own experiences – and we're pretty biased when it come to our own thoughts. Perception is an important tool in controlling behavior because it helps us determine how we can appear to others and how other people's behaviors can influence us. Your belief in yourself can affect your perception and can in turn affect your outward behavior.

We may not always know exactly how people perceive us since many will not say these things out loud, but we can make our own conclusions based on our perception of their behavior. Do they come close when they speak to you or do they try to move away? Do they smile and interact with you or do they seem withdrawn? Do you use these thoughts when you perceive people and their behaviors? It is likely you form some of the same conclusions and determine how to respond to the behaviors they are displaying.

Facts vs. Emotions

The main difference between facts and emotions is that facts are based on definite results while emotions are often involuntary and one-sided. But both facts and emotions can affect our behaviors and change how we act towards others. Facts can drive a conversation and allow people to connect on a logical level. Emotions are involved in everything we do, but sometimes they can affect the impact of our behavior and the information we are talking about.

Any social situation is most likely driven with emotions, and sometimes this can cause facts to become irrelevant and even misconstrue the information given. For example, a male speaker may not be taken seriously at a feminism rally, or a group full of teachers may not listen to a group of school board members. When you recognize that emotion may be driving the situation, it's time to reflect back on the situation and rediscover the facts and figures of the information. You may have to be a leader in the group and remind everyone to focus on the facts and save the emotions for later.

Online Communication

Online communication can be a hard concept to conquer since it can cover a wide range of areas. In our ever-growing world of technology, online communication can include emails, instant chats, video calls, and even text messages. While this form of communication can be a quick and easy way to connect with someone and cut out the need to physically see them or pick up a telephone, it can cause misconceptions in the process.

It is difficult to convey feeling, emotions, or even tone in online communications, so the use of particular words is important to remember. People may not be able to hear the light-heartedness in your words or the stern demeanor in our office warnings. Additionally, online communication can often seem impersonal, since you do not have to take the time to contact someone and speak to them personally, which can cause people to feel insulted or even slighted. When possibly, speak to the person face to face or by phone in order to get your message and feelings across. Save the electronic communications for quick and impersonal messages.

Popular forms of online communication:

- Blogs

- Emails

- Online memo

- Instant messaging

- Video or text chats

Listen and Watch More

One of the best ways to monitor your behavior and the behavior of others is to learn to listen and watch more than you participate. When listening to others talk, focus on their words, not necessarily the person saying them. Don't get caught up in one or two things they say and try to stay focused on the topic at hand. Even though you want to chime in, avoid making your own predictions and assumptions and continue to listen until the end. By watching and listening more, we are able to better to monitor the behaviors of other as well as our own since we are not focused mainly on ourselves. By focusing on the other person and their actions, we can develop better listening skills and catch more information than if we tried to assume it all ourselves.

Tips for better listening:

- Listen for verbal cues

- Watch for nonverbal cues

- Focus on what is being said, not the person

- Be aware of your own behaviors and reactions

Chapter 5 – Communication

Sadly, talking and listening has often been seen as a tool for simply communicating with other people, but not for building connections and networks. This assumption doesn't recognize the fact that interpersonal communication is a great tool to connect with people on a deeper level and form a connection with them. Speaking interpersonally allows both parties to feel more at ease and open up to one another. Just remember to be an active listener and watch your own body language.

Give Respect and Trust

It is a common courtesy in any conversation to treat the other person respectfully and professionally. By treating their ideas and opinions respectfully and with due consideration, you are showing respect by hearing them out, listening to them, and considering what they have to say with an open mind. When communicating with coworkers, it is important to build rapport and trust by speaking with each other respectfully and giving each other your full attention. After all, they deserved to be treated with dignity and courtesy for their thoughts and opinions. In addition, give your trust to them and let them know that you feel confident enough to speak with them openly. The motions and feelings we put out into the world will come back to us, so don't be afraid to speak openly with your coworkers. They will be impressed that you can give respect and trust so freely and appreciate the effort you are trying to make with them.

Be Consistent

Consistency is a key factor that builds interpersonal relationships. Being consistent in what we say and do shows knowledge and reliability because it helps build a familiar base to start from. People will want to communicate with you because you will become a factor they know they can trust and depend on. In addition, ensure that your actions are consistent with what you say – in other words– do what you say you'll do. If you say you will meet someone after lunch to review a report, ensure that you are there early to greet them. If you volunteered to give a speech at the next work convention, be prepared ahead of time and be ready when the day arrives. Showing you are consistent in turn shows how reliable you are and what an asset you can be for the group.

Take a few minutes to reflect back on your actions and note if they have been consistent over time. Are there behaviors you can change? What can you do differently in the future?

Always Keep Your Cool

Keeping our cool in tight or stressful situations can be tough and takes a lot of skill to make it through gracefully. It is perfectly normal to feel embarrassed or hurt when someone does something you don't like, such as speaking rudely to you or pointing out a mistake you made. Our first instinct is to possibly lash out at them or try to retaliate by hurting them in return. But the key to strong and professional communication is to keep your cool at all times and not let the negative feelings take over. When something happens that may send you over the edge, take a minute to reflect on what was said and what happened. If needed, you should step away for a few moments to compose yourself. Don't deny the other person their opinion, but let them know how you feel and how it affects you. Kinder coworkers will back track their statements and try to address the problem in less negative terms. If the coworker is unwilling to give respect, realize that their opinion may not be worth the fight.

Tips for keeping your cool:

- Try not to take words personally

- Stop and reflect *what* was said, not *how* it was said

- Make a note to learn from this experience

- Ask yourself if the person had reason for what was said – if so, what can you do to change it?

Observing Body Language

Body language can speak volumes between people, even if it does not have words to accompany it. Many times people may say one message, but their body language can say another, meaning they may not be truthful in what they say. By observing and becoming more aware of body language and what it might mean, we can learn to read people more easily and understand some of their body movements. By better understanding their movements, you can be better prepared to communicate with them, while at the same time better understanding the body language you may be conveying to them. Even though there are times that we can send mixed messages, we can try to get our point across using certain behaviors. Our body language affects how we act with others and how we react to them, as well as how they can react to ours.

Chapter 6 – Social Cues

Social cues are verbal or non-verbal hints that let us know what someone maybe thinking or feeling. When in a social situation, it is important to keep an eye out for these social cues and ensure our behavior isn't contributing to them. While some cues can be obvious, other may be very subtle, so we must train ourselves to be able to recognize them when they do appear.

Recognize Social Situations

Social situations are not a 'one size fits all' situation. Because the people in each situation are different, we must learn to adapt ourselves to this ever-changing group – and know how to handle them. This does not mean we have to change who we are or hide our own personality, but rather we can change how we present ourselves around other people. Some of the best hints we can use are the ones we get from other people around you. How are they behaving? How are they 'working through' the event? Do you know all of them? Are there faces you do not recognize? With this information in mind, determine what type of social situation you may be in. Is this a formal gathering? Is it a business meeting or function with coworkers? Maybe a few friends catching a bite to eat? The key is to recognize your surroundings and the people involved to help determine how to present yourself.

Questions to ask in a social situation:

- "What is the gathering for?"

- "Who is present?"

- "Do we share common interests?"

The Eyes Have It

Not all cues from others can be seen right and may be well hidden, but the eyes will always give them away. Without blatantly staring at a person (of course), try to observe how they are looking at you and others. Do certain words or phrases make them blink more or dart their eyes in another direction? Are they staying focused on a subject for a long period of time? Unfortunately, the eyes cannot lie – often. Many feelings or behaviors we try to hide in ourselves will often be shown through the eyes. Common eye behaviors such as rolling the eyes or looking around frequently can be signs of boredom or discomfort. If a person looks at you while talking or moves their eyebrows while listening to you talk, this can be a sign of interest or curiosity. But since these feelings may not be said out loud, or even gestured, it is a key tool to remember when gauging the people around you.

Common eye behaviors:

- Eye rolling

- Blinking too much or too little

- Wandering eyes; not looking directly at a person

- Long blinks

Non-Verbal Cues

It has been said that non-verbal communication is the most powerful form of communication since it can expand beyond voice, tone, and even words. It accounts for over 90% of our communication methods. Although the differences in non-verbal communication can be different in certain situations (amount of personal space or use of hand gestures), most cues can send the same message across the board. Nonverbal cues can include facial expressions, body movements, eye movement, and various gestures and usually are not associated with supported words or phrases.

Common non-verbal cues include folding the arms, gripping or moving hands while speaking, rolling the eyes and even misusing the tone of voice. Do you notice these gestures when speaking with people around you? When thinking of your behavior, do you find yourself making any of these gestures when you are in a social situation? If so, think of ways you can try to eliminate some of them and replace them with more welcoming or outgoing gestures instead.

Common non-verbal cues:

- Folding the arms

- Looking around frequently

- Tapping the feet or clasping hands

- Fidgeting

- Moving closer/farther away

Verbal Cues

Verbal cues are cues that we are more likely to pick up on and notice right away. They are usually done with some sort of emphasis or tone that causes an effect within us, and is mostly likely to stick with us in the future. Phrases such as "Did you see the new *rules* in the handbook?" or "I *can't* wait to see the projections for this week" add emphasis to certain words to stress a point or effect. Other verbal cues can include appropriate pauses when speaking, pitch, or volume of the voice or even speaking too slowly or quickly. These are cues that we can control and use with our voices (hence the term *verbal*) to get a message across.

When in a social situation, listen to those around you and determine what verbal cues you can pick up on. Do they sound positive or negative? Do they appropriately portray the message being sent? Do you find yourself using these verbal cues on others? Maybe you emphasized the wrong word or spoke in a higher pitch when trying to speak with a group of people. When we can recognize these cues in others and learn to adapt ourselves to them, we can learn to identify them in ourselves and ensure that we are not putting the wrong message out there.

Common verbal cues:

- Voice tone or pitch

- Word emphasis

- Volume

- Uncomfortable pauses or word inserts

Social cues can often enhance, or even downplay, what is being said or portrayed in a situation. But the social cue needs to be interpreted in the right manner for it to better a social situation – not make it worse. People who are better equipped to identify and understand these social cues are more likely to act appropriately to them, and will be better prepared to respond to them and adapt their behavior.

Spectrum of Cues

As in all situations, there is always a possibility for going to one extreme to the other without having any middle ground in between. For social cues, it can be a fairly wide spectrum with plenty of variations. On one side of the spectrum, a person can be very obvious with their cues, such as speaking very loudly or making very large and awkward hand gestures. These types of cues are easy to spot and can often make people feel uncomfortable right away. On the other hand, there are cues that are more subtle and can often be missed if not recognized right away, such as excessive eye blinking or adding a tone to their words.

Unfortunately, these types of cues may go unnoticed and can portray the wrong message when they may not be intended to. They key point is being able to recognize each side of this spectrum and the different ways a social cue can go wrong and right at the same time. When you learn the extremes they can reach, you're better equipped to catch the cues in between and adapt your behavior faster.

Review and Reflect

It's a natural behavior to want to react to a cue we may recognize and want to confront right away. Are you bored? Did I offend you? Did you understand? But these approaches are not the best solution to connect with people and better understand their behavior. When you notice a social cue, such as someone rolling their eyes or speaking in a shrill voice at you, take a moment to stop and review the action. Take notice if it is being directed at you or if others around you are subject to it as well. Does the behavior continue? Maybe the behavior was a onetime occurrence?

Reflect on what you can do to adapt yourself to the situation. Was there something you said to trigger this feeling? Does this person have something they want to share? Or maybe you just need to take a step back from this person. Sometimes they need a moment to review and reflect as well, and may need some personal space to do it. Whatever your results, remember to refrain from jumping to conclusions about the cues we encounter. Always take a minute to two before responding with your own actions.

Being Adaptable and Flexible

Even though there are times we can pick up on these social cues, we may be able to change them or even get away from them as soon as we'd like. These are the times we must learn to be flexible and adapt to the situation. We all know that not all situations will be comfortable for us and we may need to find a way to adapt until it's over. Sometimes the room can have more people than we are comfortable with or maybe the other visitors are sending cues of boredom or annoyance, but don't let these cues sink you. Be flexible to the group and reflect on what you can do to help the situation. Try to start a conversation with people that seem distant or unsure. Lead by example and speak in lower pitches or in casual tones. Many times the people around you will catch onto the cues you are sending out and will become adaptable as well. This great trick doesn't always work in all situations, but it is one way we can help ourselves adapt and manage through a difficult situation.

Personal Space

Edward Hall was one of the first people to define and characterize the space around us – our different level of spaces. The outer most space around us is our public space, such as in a large room. Coming in closer is our social space, such as talking with a group of friends. The next inward space is our personal space, which is usually within arms' reach of us. This space is usually on reserve for 'invitation-only', meaning we do not like for people to be in our personal space unless we initiate it and welcome them over.

In social situations, this can be a hard thing to maintain. The key is to refrain from being rude to someone who may have encroached on your space. If this person is too close, take a few steps to the side instead of backwards, which creates subtle distance and doesn't appear as though you are backing away. If you must leave a group of people, or even just one, that are too close, always excuse yourself politely and move to an open area. If possible, take a few steps around the room every so often, which keeps you mobile and doesn't allow for crowding. Remember, this is the time to be adaptable, so you may need to be flexible with your surroundings to feel more at ease.

Tips for keeping your personal space personal:

- Excuse yourself politely when leaving a group

- Step to the side a step or two to create subtle distance

- Walk often or roam about the area – if possible

- Opt for a handshake when greeting people – it allows for the other person to stay at arm's length

- Be aware of cultural differences in personal space

Chapter 7 – Conversation Skills

Conversation is like an adhesive that can bring people together. It can make friends, create networks, and even seal a deal. But it can have the opposite effect when used in the wrong way. Some key points about holding a conversation include the topic, the tone, and even presentation. Only you are familiar with how to work on these aspects, conversation in social situations will become second nature.

Current Events

Discussing current events can be a great skill to build conversation and become engaged in the real world around us. Tragic current events, such as war or weather disasters, can bring in many members to a conversation and can share empathy and sorrow among people. Of course more pleasant events, such as economic upswing and the cost of gas going down can be a more uplifting line of topics to discuss and create a lighter atmosphere. Discussing what is going on in the world allows for group members to connect on many levels. After all, we live here and we see what's going on! But be aware of current events that can cross into sensitive topics such as politics or religion, since these can offend some people and cause tension among a group.

Conversation Topics

Sometimes when we speak among other people in social situations, the lines of safe conversation topics can become blurry. We can become too comfortable and begin talking about subjects that can seem fine to some people, but can be offensive or rude to others. It is usually recommended to stick with topics that are considered 'safe' for everyone, such as common work areas or hobbies. Some other safe topics include sporting events, television or movies and even forms of travel. These can help people connections and friendships without crossing into dangerous territories. Some infamous topics to avoid include religion, gossip, risqué jokes, and the government/politics, since these can cause tension and arguments among group members, even if it was not the intention.

If all else fails, you can always talk about the weather!

Topics to avoid in a group:

- Religion

- Politics

- Personal health

- Prejudice topics (racism, sexism, etc.), including jokes

Cues to Watch For

As we've come to learn, we're not psychic and can't always predict what other people are thinking. This is why it is important to learn about verbal and nonverbal cues to look and listen for when in a social situation. Remember the nonverbal cues such as crossing the arms or turning their heads away to signal signs of discomfort or disinterest. These can be signs to change the current subject or recognize that something inappropriate was probably said. However, cues such as full smiles or open hands can be positive in nature and can signal approval and happiness.

Many cues that are given are from the subconscious are not always shared on purpose, especially if some feels offended or angry, in which they may not want to express out loud. So while in the midst of a conversation, look around at the people talking and the people listening. Do you see any of the typical cues, such as eye rolling, loud speaking, turned away bodies or inappropriate laughter? If so, what can you do to change the situation or even adapt yourself to it?

Cues to keep an eye out for:

- Cues signaling boredom or annoyance

- Cues signaling anger or offense

- Cues signaling different types of body language – whether open or closed

- Cues signaling for interest or comfort

Give People Your Attention

Whether you're in a conversation with just one person, a few people, or even a large group, it is important for you to give them your attention. It shows your respect for the person, or people, talking and that you really value what they are saying. When listening to other people, nod your head and make eye contact with them to let them know they have your attention and that you are listening. This can make people feel more at ease with you and make them not only put their trust in you, but feel more confident when speaking with you. If you know a head of time that you will be in a group or be speaking with others, remember to turn off your phone or set it to vibrate, so it will not be a distraction. The emails or notices can usually wait until after your conversation.

Tips to remember:

- Make eye contact

- Nod and show facial movements

- Ask questions or make a follow up comment

- Remove distractions, such as cell phones

Chapter 8 – Body Language

Body language is a form of language that relies on body movements as gestures. It accounts for over 90% of the language we use in society – the other 10% consisting of actual words or phrases. It can provide cues and hints about how the other person is feeling and thinking. Learning to read body language is an important lesson to know since people may not always simply say what is on their mind, but will definitely show it in their movements.

Be Aware of Your Movements

Unless the room is covered in mirrors, we may not always be aware of the body language we are displaying to people around us. Since the majority of body language is nonverbal, we cannot always control what we show and what we are 'saying', so we must learn to be aware of our own movements and gestures to prevent any miscommunications. Some tips to try out on your own are to look at yourself in a reflective surface, such as a mirror or a piece of glass, and practice saying things from a conversation. Do you show any signs of body language – and what are they? When in the room, listen to what other people are saying when they talk to you. Don't put up defense barriers and block them out. Look at the way they act or behave when they are around you or speak directly to you. Their body language can often let you know how you are coming across and let you know what you may be putting out into the room, even if you are not aware of it.

It's Not What You Say – It's How You Say It

When we rely on our words alone and open our mouths to let them out, we can accidentally let fly all sorts of meanings and phrases that were never meant to come out. Linguistic tools such as tone, emphasis, and even pitch can make even the simplest or nicest phrase come out very wrong. When we speak, the emphasis on certain words comes naturally, which can seem off-putting to others and can lead to a confused message. It can often lead them to question if that is what you meant to say or if you just didn't know what you were trying to say to begin with.

Practice saying the following phrase with tone and emphasis on a different word each time:

- *"**I'd** like to help you work on your presentations."*

- "I'd like to help you *work on* your presentations."

- "I'd like to help you work on your *presentations*."

Do you hear the different messages that the same phrase can have with different words stressed and tones implied? The words we say only make up half of our message – the rest is in how you say it.

Open vs. Closed Body Language

Our body language can be like a traffic light to the people around us. Open body language can signal a green light for people to approach you and engage in conversations with you. However, closed body language can signal a red light and make people want to keep their distance from you while they can. Open body language includes gestures such as having open hands and palms, making eye contact, and reaching out to greet someone. This can also you seem more persuasive when speaking with other people and gain their trust. Closed body language such as crossing the arms, turning the head away and constantly fidgeting are much less inviting, and will not get other people to come around. This kind of body language can make you seem defensive and withholding from those around you. If you wish to communicate well with others, it is important to realize how to use (and not use) your body to speak out.

Examples of Open Body Language	Examples of Closed Body Language
Feet facing forward	Looking away or around the room
Smiling face	Crossing the arms or legs
Open palms	Turning your body away
Making eye contact	Rolling the eyes or blinking excessively

Communicate with Power

Effective communication is key in any situation. When you communicate with others, you want it to be a powerful message that they will take away with them when you part ways. No one wants their message to come across as week and easily forgotten. Before you even begin to form words, think about what you want to say, and how you want your message to come across. Make notes of any wrongful tones or emphasis might be used and prevent it. When you are done speaking, listen to what the other person has to say and show signs of active listening, such as nodding your head or asking follow up questions. Turn your body to the other person and give them your full attention during the session. As always, remove any distractions that can incur the wrong body language, such as checking a ringing phone or being distracted while checking emails.

Tips for communicating with power:

- Think before you speak

- Be an active listener

- Watch for verbal and nonverbal cues

- Be aware of your body language

Chapter 9 – Building Rapport

Rapport is used in the business world to build professional relationships and networks. It helps gain confidence and trust in other people and makes them feel more at ease. When in social situations, this can include simple techniques such as mirroring and sharing common interests. Building rapport early on can help you be successful later in business and create less awkward moments in social situations.

Take the High Road

Building rapport is about standing out and standing above others around you to make connections and networks with various people. While this can seem like an aggressive gesture, it is actually just the opposite. Taking the high road is being humble and putting others before yourself. Don't treat the situation like a competition, but rather more of a showcase. Show others that you can be a great listener as well as a contributor to a team or group. While others are scrambling around you to show off their talents and skills to come out as the 'top dog', take the road less taken and have a lower profile to display. Offer your input and take interest in what the other person is saying. By showing you can stand out over the others without trying to crush them shows that you can display great skills without having to put others down in the process, which benefits the entire group. Remember, building rapport is about building connections- not destroying them.

Forget About Yourself

When you want to build rapport with another person, or group, the key element is to actually take yourself out of the equation. Although you have things to say and contribute, spend more time listening to what they have to say and ask follow up questions to expand on their ideas. Yes, you know you have great opinions and ideas and want to share them with the world, but this is not the time. Building rapport requires you to develop an honest interest in another party besides yourself. Become interested in the people around you and what they do and stand for. When people feel that you care about their lives and what they do, they are more inclined to open up and share more, opening the gates to build stronger connections and longer relationships.

Key points to remember:

- Be an active listener

- Show interest in their ideas and thoughts

- Ask for follow up information

- Offer opinions as needed, but focus on them

Remembering People

When we meet new people, sometimes the names or faces can become a blur. Most people are great at remembering one or the other, but rarely both. But rapport depends on being able to recall a person at a later time over many encounters. One of the main reasons we forget a person's name or face is because we are not truly listening or paying attention when we are being introduced. Don't be nervous and put your mind at ease so that you can easily register the person's face and hearing their name with it. When you look at the person, look for any features that stand out, such as hair color, facial features, scars or even the use of makeup. Remembering a key characteristic while fully listening to their name will help keep them associated in your brain to retrieve at a later date when needed.

Tips to remember name and faces:

- Say their name immediately after hearing it

- Don't be afraid to ask them to repeat their name

- Associate a gesture with their greeting, such as a handshake or smile

- Remember distinct features

Ask Good Questions

You cannot expect to get anywhere with people if you do not know more about them and form a connection with them. One of the best ways to start building this connection is to ask good questions that allow them to share their pearls of wisdom and what they have come to know over time. In turn, they will usually ask for your opinions or thoughts after they have shared, pulling you into to create a network of ideas. The key is asking questions about them and their company, which gives them plenty of area to talk about themselves. Ask open-ended questions that pertain to what they do or don't like about their area and what kind of advice they would offer newcomers. Try to avoid simple yes or no questions, or questions that can make you seem as though you are encroaching on their territory. You're trying to build a bridge between people, not burning it behind you.

Sample questions to ask:

- "What do you enjoy most about _____?"

- "What kind of advice would you offer someone like me?"

- "What are some of your accomplishments with the company?"

- "What is one thing you would want everyone to know about your business?"

Additional Titles

The 90 Minute Guide series of books covers a variety of general business skills and are intended to be completed in 90 minutes or less. It is an effective way for building your skill set and can be used to acquire professional development units needed by project managers and other industries to maintain their certification. For the availability of titles please see

https://www.silvercitypublications.com/shop/.

No. 1 - Appreciative Inquiry

No. 2 - Assertiveness and Self Control

No. 3 - Attention Management

No. 4 - Body Language Basics

No. 5 - Business Acumen

No. 6 - Business and Etiquette

No. 7 - Change Management

No. 8 - Coaching and Mentoring

No. 9 - Communications Strategies

No. 10 - Conflict Resolution